The World of Plants

by Michael L. Macceca

Science Contributor
Sally Ride Science

Science Consultants
Thomas R. Ciccone, Science Educator
Ronald Edwards, Science Educator

First hardcover edition published in 2010 by
Compass Point Books
151 Good Counsel Drive
P.O. Box 669
Mankato, MN 56002-0669

Editor: Anthony Wacholtz
Designer: Heidi Thompson
Editorial Contributor: Robin Doak
Media Researcher: Svetlana Zhurkin
Production Specialist: Jane Klenk

Library of Congress Cataloging-in-Publication Data
Macceca, Michael L.
 The world of plants / by Michael L. Macceca.
    p. cm.—(Mission, science)
 Includes index.
 ISBN 978-0-7565-4304-4 (library binding)
 1. Plants—Juvenile literature. 2. Botany—Juvenile literature.
 I.Title. II. Series.
 QK49.M25 2010
 580—dc22   2009034853

Visit Compass Point Books on the Internet at *www.compasspointbooks.com*
or e-mail your request to *custserv@compasspointbooks.com*

Table of Contents

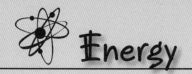

Energy

Energy is the force that powers the universe. It makes the stars shine, keeps the planets spinning, warms Earth, and makes plants grow. Every living thing on Earth needs energy to survive and function.

Energy comes in many forms. We use energy from the wind, oceans, volcanoes, and materials that come from the earth, such as oil and coal. The element uranium, found in many types of rocks, is used to create nuclear energy.

All life on Earth needs energy to survive.

Plants use the sun's energy to grow.

Did You Know?

Broccoli crowns are really the flowers of the plant. So are strawberries. Both are good to eat and good for you, too.

For plants and animals, the most important energy source is solar energy from the sun. Endless amounts of energy stream through space to Earth in the form of solar radiation. Plants store this heat and light energy, using it later to grow and reproduce by making seeds, flowers, or fruit.

Animals take advantage of this conversion of energy by harvesting and eating the plants.

Solar Energy Powers the Water Cycle

Energy can be used in many ways. When you walk, run, or even shiver, you are using energy that was stored by your body when you ate food.

Solar energy is the main energy source that powers our environment. The sun's heat causes water to evaporate into the sky. When the water vapor cools, it condenses and forms clouds. Precipitation falls from the clouds and is collected in lakes, rivers, and streams. Eventually it evaporates. The water cycle is repeated over and over. It helps make life on Earth possible.

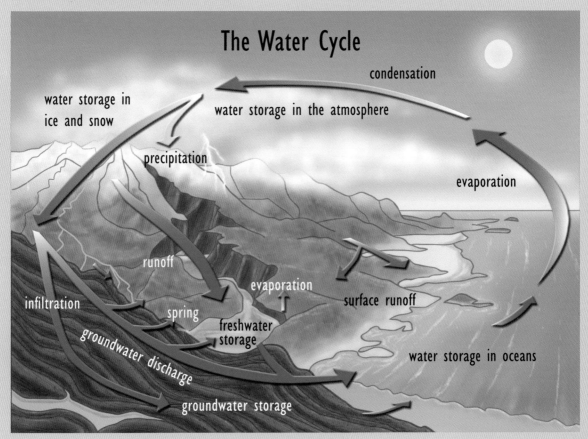

The Water Cycle

condensation

water storage in ice and snow

water storage in the atmosphere

precipitation

evaporation

runoff

evaporation

surface runoff

infiltration

spring

freshwater storage

groundwater discharge

water storage in oceans

groundwater storage

Energy and Electricity

Solar energy can also be used to make electricity. Wind currents, created by the heating and cooling of Earth, turn wind turbines that make electricity. Water that falls to Earth is collected behind dams. It is then used to make hydroelectric power. Solar energy panels use cells that are similar to batteries. The cells change the sun's rays to electricity. Electricity created in one of these ways is called green energy. Making it does not pollute the environment. The energy source is also renewable.

Most electricity today, however, is generated by burning fossil fuels. They include coal and oil, which are made from ancient plants. Electricity can also be made by a nuclear reactor. But electricity made in both of these ways creates harmful pollution.

What Is a Plant?

Plants are living things. They grow in almost every environment on Earth. They grow on the tops of mountains and in the middle of deserts. Some grow on the icy tundra, while others grow in the water. But no matter where they are, plants need sun, water, air, and food to grow.

Most plants have three distinct parts: roots, stems, and leaves. Each part performs vital tasks that are needed for the plant to process energy and grow. Plants change the energy in sunlight into food by a process called photosynthesis.

Plant Clothes

You might be wearing plants right now! The plant most commonly used for clothing is cotton. More than 23 million tons (20.7 metric tons) of cotton are grown each year around the world. China, the United States, and India grow more than half the world's cotton.

Other plants used to make clothing include flax, hemp, and ramie. Scientists continue to look for new ways to use plants. They have recently developed ways to make clothes out of bamboo, corn, soybeans, and even banana stems.

Roots

Plants are anchored to the ground by their roots. Without roots, plants would blow away in windy weather or wash away during rainstorms. Another important job of roots is absorbing nutrients from the soil and transporting them to the rest of the plant. Roots extend down into the soil and absorb water there. In the water are minerals from the surrounding soil. Some minerals come from plants that have died and are rotting.

Roots have many tiny hairs that help keep the plant in the soil.

Unusual Roots

The banyan starts life when a bird drops its seed in a crack of another tree. As the banyan grows, its roots wrap around the host tree and reach down toward the ground. The roots can grow to be as big as tree trunks. They can spread over large areas of ground. One famous banyan tree in Hawaii shades two-thirds of an acre.

When a plant dies, it decomposes. All the nutrients that are stored in it return to the soil. More nutrients come from decomposing animals and microorganisms. New plants use these nutrients to grow. Lawns and gardens need these nutrients. Since we don't often keep decomposing plants in our yards, we have to add fertilizer. It has all the nutrients that plants need.

Decomposing plant stalks ⬆
and leaves in soil

13

Stems

Stems hold up and support the leaves, flowers, and fruit of a plant. They also contain the system of tiny tubes that carry water and nutrients throughout the plant. These tubes are called xylem and phloem. Xylem carries nutrients from the roots to the leaves. Phloem carries food from the leaves to other parts of the plant. Stems also store nutrients for later use.

As a plant matures and grows older, its stems grow longer and thicker.

Over time, the outside of the stem becomes rough and thick, like bark. This helps protect the plant. Many plants grow spikes or thorns. These help keep the plants from being eaten by animals.

Inside a Stem

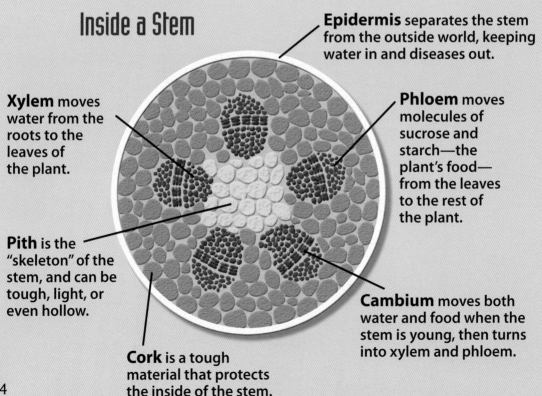

Epidermis separates the stem from the outside world, keeping water in and diseases out.

Xylem moves water from the roots to the leaves of the plant.

Phloem moves molecules of sucrose and starch—the plant's food—from the leaves to the rest of the plant.

Pith is the "skeleton" of the stem, and can be tough, light, or even hollow.

Cambium moves both water and food when the stem is young, then turns into xylem and phloem.

Cork is a tough material that protects the inside of the stem.

Sugar Stalks

Sugar comes from a stalk or stem. Juice is squeezed from the cut stalks of the sugarcane plant. This liquid is then dried. Crystals of pure, raw sugar are left over.

Sugar was once very rare and valuable. It did not grow well in Europe. On his second voyage to the Americas, Christopher Columbus took sugarcane cuttings with him to see how they would grow in the New World. The plants thrived in the lush, tropical climate of the Caribbean. Sugar became one of the most important and profitable trade goods from the New World. It was even called "white gold." Sugar also comes from the sugar beet, which is grown in cooler climates.

Leaves

Leaves are an important part of every plant. During photosynthesis, food for the plant is made inside the flat part of the leaf called the blade. The food passes through tiny tubes called veins throughout the leaf. Food is carried from the veins to the stalk, which connects the leaf to the stem.

Leaves come in many shapes and sizes, depending partly upon the climate where they live. They adapt to climate over time. Leaves on pine trees are called needles. Leaves on palm trees are called fronds. Some leaves are soft and hairy, while others are smooth and shiny.

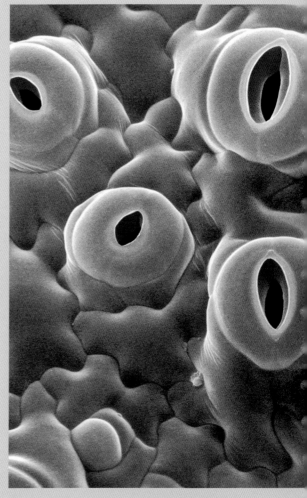

Leaves can be found in many shapes and sizes.

Medicine From Plants

For thousands of years, people in many cultures have made medicines from plants. The study of this type of medicine is called herbology. Leaves, stems, and roots from certain plants and trees are used. They are mixed with other ingredients to target a certain illness. Sometimes the mixture is brewed into a tea, which the patient drinks. Herbal remedies of the past have used garlic, mint, thyme, and cinnamon.

Many botanical medicines are still used today. Experts say one of every four modern medicines came from an herbal cure, including aspirin.

Stomata are pores found on the leaf surface. They control the exchange of gases from the leaf to the atmosphere.

Growth

Plants use the food they make to grow new stems and leaves. As a result, the plants get bigger and taller. As they grow, they stretch toward the sun so they can make more food. Plants never stop growing. Some grow slowly, and some grow fast. They continue to grow until they are killed by climate conditions, disease, fire, animals, or humans.

Plants also use their food to make seeds for new plants. The seeds are scattered near and far by the wind, birds, and animals. This is how plants reproduce.

Did You Know?

Redwood trees are among the tallest trees in the world. They can reach more than 360 feet (109 meters) in height.

Trees: A Renewable Resource?

A resource is a supply of something that meets our needs. A renewable resource can be replaced as fast as it is consumed. Plants can either grow back on their own or be replanted. Corn is a renewable resource. We eat it and feed it to farm animals. We get sweetener and cooking oil from it. We also convert it into fuel and cloth. Farmers plant enough corn every year to meet our needs.

Trees are cut down for use as lumber, which is used to build houses, furniture, and other things. It's also used to make paper. Until recently, trees were thought to be an endlessly renewable resource. Whole mountains were stripped of their trees. This was done by a practice called clear-cutting. Then people realized that the trees couldn't grow back without our help. Now the lumber industry practices selective cutting. Only some trees are removed from a forest, which leaves plenty of trees to repopulate the area.

Photosynthesis

Plants make the food they need to survive and grow using a process called photosynthesis. It takes place in a plant's leaves. Each leaf is made of cells that are filled with a green substance called chlorophyll. The chlorophyll molecules are like tiny factories. They convert the sun's rays to energy. They also give leaves their green color.

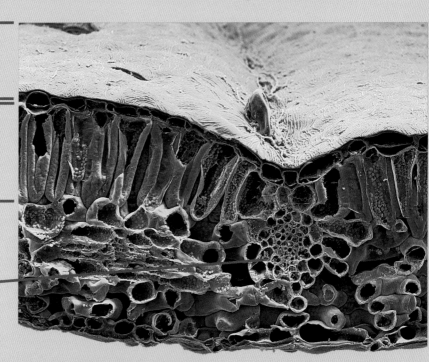

upper surface of the leaf

cells containing chlorophyll

vascular tubes

No Fungi Needed

Some plants don't use photosynthesis to make food. These plants grow on fungi and steal their food. For that reason, the plants are also known as parasites. Some types of orchids are parasites.

Enough for All

Photosynthesis takes in carbon dioxide and releases oxygen. This is a good thing for us. Animals need to breathe in oxygen to turn food into energy. We breathe out carbon dioxide. Using oxygen to turn food into energy is called respiration. Plants respire, too. But they only use a little of the oxygen that they make. Fortunately there's plenty left over for us!

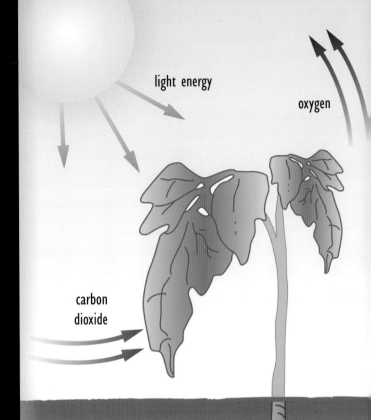

light energy

oxygen

carbon
dioxide

water

During photosynthesis, plants use solar energy to convert carbon dioxide from air and hydrogen from water into a type of food called carbohydrates. Most of the oxygen from the water is not needed by the plants. This leftover oxygen is released into the air.

Without photosynthesis, life on Earth would not be possible. The oxygen released by plants during photosynthesis is used by humans and other animals with every breath they take.

Underwater Oxygen Makers

If you went swimming in the ocean, you would see some fish and other sea creatures. You would also see organisms that look like plants. One kind of seaweed, called kelp, grows close to the shore. Kelp is green and leafy. You might think it is a plant, but it is actually a kind of organism called algae. Other algae are so small you can hardly see them. Algae and seaweed photosynthesize just as plants on land do.

When algae make food, they release oxygen into the water. Fish use some of the oxygen to breathe. Some of the oxygen is released into the air. Since Earth is mostly covered with oceans, many scientists believe algae are the most important source of oxygen on the planet.

Did You Know?

Coral is not a plant. It is a whole colony of small animals called polyps. They live inside the hard, protective shells that they make. The shells are what we call coral.

Seaweed! Yum!

Seaweed is used in many foods we eat. It is used to thicken things or make them gooey. Toothpaste, yogurt, and your favorite candies all have seaweed in them. The most common use of seaweed is in ice cream.

Protecting Plants From Pests

Have you ever bitten into an apple and found a worm? The worm is one of many pests that can damage or destroy plants. People grow plants to eat the food they produce. But other living things also want to eat the plants. We can build fences to keep animal pests like rabbits and deer away, but that doesn't work for smaller pests like worms and insects. There are even some pests that are invisible to the naked eye. These tiny organisms are called microbes, and they can cause diseases in plants.

To protect their crops, farmers use chemicals called pesticides that are toxic to pests. Some chemicals can be injected as a gas directly into the soil. Others are sprayed on the crops from an airplane. In some cases, seeds are coated with a pesticide before they are planted.

Organic farmers are different. They do not use pesticides. They believe this makes their food safer to eat. But the food is more expensive than nonorganic food, because the pests eat their share.

Ant Farms

Leaf-cutter ants in Central and South America grow their own crops. They bring leaf cuttings to their nests. Then they feed these pieces to their "fungus gardens." The ants keep the fungus free from pests and mold. Then the ants harvest the fungus for food.

Plants are found in almost every kind of environment on Earth. There are plants that survive in the snow near the North Pole. There are plants that live in the hottest desert. Wherever they are found, plants are prepared for their environment. Over thousands of years, plants have slowly changed so they are perfectly suited to the places they grow.

An example of a plant that has adapted to its environment is the palm tree. Palms are tall and have a flexible trunk. When a tropical storm blows through, palm trees sway back and forth, but they usually don't break. It took millions of years for this kind of palm tree to develop. Each new tree was a little different from the tree before it. Palms that weren't flexible broke under the high winds. The trees that were flexible survived. Their seeds grew into the next trees, which were also flexible. Eventually they became the palm trees we know today.

Did You Know?

Not all plants need soil to grow, but they still need the nutrients that soil provides. Some plants can be grown in a vase with water alone, as long as the water is rich in nutrients. Some orchids can be grown this way.

Many Kinds of Leaves

Have you noticed that each type of tree has leaves of a particular shape and size? Leaves are the part of a plant that is most exposed to its environment. For this reason, you can see how a tree or other plant has adapted to its environment by looking at its leaves. A cactus' leaves, for example, are its spines. They have adapted to the heat and sun in the desert.

Pine needles are also a modified version of leaves. The length of the needles and the number per bundle vary, depending on the climate where a pine grows. The colder and dryer it is, the shorter the needle.

The pinyon pine has single ▲ needles that are very short. It lives where the climate is cold and dry.

The ponderosa pine has ▲ bundles of three long needles and lives where there is plenty of water and warm summers.

27

Plants are a vital part of our world. Animals breathe the oxygen that plants make and release carbon dioxide that plants use. During photosynthesis, plants produce food to help them grow. Animals that eat plants also benefit from the food.

Plants have adapted over millions of years to live in almost every environment on Earth. People have also adapted some plants for use as food. Farmers grow crops in very large amounts so they can supply whole cities of people with food.

Next time you relax under a tree, remember that the tree is doing a lot of work. The roots are taking in water and nutrients. These nutrients are being carried through the stems to the leaves and made into food for the tree. The tree makes more leaves, and maybe nuts or fruits, as it continues to grow toward the sky.

Some plants, such as the Venus flytrap, get nutrients from insects they catch.

We benefit from plants every day, ▲
whether it's getting the food we eat
or finding a shady spot under a tree.

29

Transportation With Plants

We can't see plants grow because they grow so slowly. We do know that plants absorb water and nutrients from the soil. These substances are then carried from the roots to the stems and leaves.

To learn more about plants, do an experiment that shows how water is transported through a plant.

Materials

- beaker or tall glass

- water

- red food coloring

- stalk of celery with leaves

Procedure

1   Fill the beaker or glass with water and add red food coloring until it is dark red.

2   Place the stalk of celery into the beaker with the leaves sticking out, and let it sit for a while.

3   After some time, the red water will flow through the plant's stem and turn the tips of the leaves red.

4   Slice the stalk in half. You will see the small tubes that carry water and nutrients to the leaves.

Conclusion

1   Describe what you observe in the celery. Why do you see what you see?

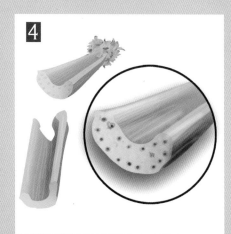

2   What do you think would happen if you turned the stalk upside down and placed the leaves in the colored water? Why?

3   The longer the celery remains in the water, the darker it becomes. Why do you think this is so?

Important People in Botany

Aristotle (384 B.C.–322 B.C.)
Greek philosopher who collected a large amount of information about plants and animals and has been called the world's first important biologist

Charles Barnes (1858–1910)
American plant biologist who first suggested using the term photosynthesis to describe the way a plant converts sunlight and nutrients into food

Hieronymus Bock (1498–1554)
German scientist known as one of the three founding fathers of botany; noted for beginning the modern practice of sorting plants by their relation or resemblance to one another

Otto Brunfels (c. 1488–1534)
German scientist known as one of the founding fathers of botany; he studied and described many types of plants

Luther Burbank (1849–1926)
American plant breeder who developed more than 800 new types of plants, including fruits, flowers, grains, grasses, and vegetables

George Washington Carver (c. 1865–1943)
American botanist who discovered many uses for peanuts and other plants and taught modern agricultural methods, including crop rotation, to university students and farmers

Jane Colden (1724–1766)
The first female American botanist, she collected and categorized more than 300 types of plants from the lower Hudson River Valley in New York

Abu al-Dinawari (c. 815–896)
Arabic scientist who first described the phases of plant growth from birth to death; also experimented with various types of soil

Henri Dutrochet (1776–1847)
French scientist who recognized that chlorophyll was necessary for photosynthesis

Leonhart Fuchs (1501–1566)
German scientist considered to be one of the three founding fathers of botany; the tropical flowering plant fuchsia is named for him

Nehemiah Grew (1641–1712)
English scientist who studied the anatomy of vegetables; published the *Anatomy of Plants* in 1682

Alexander von Humboldt (1769–1859)
German scientist who pioneered the idea of writing about plants based on their location, also known as botanical geography; known as the father of ecology

Jan Ingenhousz (1730–1799)
Dutch-born English scientist who discovered the process by which green plants use sunlight to convert water, carbon dioxide, and minerals into food and oxygen; it was later called photosynthesis

Anton van Leeuwenhoek (1632–1723)
Dutch scientist known as the father of the microscope; examined the internal structures of plants and showed how sap moves through their tubelike parts

Justus von Liebig (1803–1873)
German chemist who was a pioneer in organic chemistry; known as the father of the fertilizer industry for his discovery that nitrogen is an important plant nutrient; developed the modern laboratory method of teaching science

Carl Linnaeus (1707–1778)
Swedish botanist who divided the plant kingdom into 25 classes and created the first logical and systematic way to classify all living things; after some changes, it became the standard system scientists use today

Alice Lounsberry (1872–1949)
American botanist and author of several books on plants, including *A Guide to the Wild Flowers*

Barbara McClintock (1902–1992)
American geneticist whose study of corn revealed that some genes can move within the chromosomes of cells, a discovery that earned her a Nobel Prize in 1983

Joseph Priestley (1733–1804)
English scientist who showed that plants in sunlight give off oxygen and "restore" air that lacks oxygen because of burning or the breathing of animals

Ellis Rowan (1847–1922)
Australian botanical artist known for her detailed and accurate drawings of various plants; she created illustrations for three books written by American botanist Alice Lounsberry

Julius von Sachs (1832–1897)
German botanist who founded the scientific study of plant physiology (how plant processes work)

Dunkinfield Henry Scott (1854–1934)
English scientist who pioneered the study of fossil plants

Jean Senebier (1742–1809)
Swiss botanist who discovered that green plants, using light, take in carbon dioxide and give off oxygen

Theophrastus (c. 372 B.C.–c. 287 B.C.)
Greek philosopher who named and classified many plants based on information gathered by his teacher, Aristotle; he is considered the father of botany

Eugenius Warming (1841–1924)
Danish botanist who was the first person to describe the science now known as ecology, the study of living things in relation to their environment

Karl Wilhelm von Nägeli (1817–1891)
Swiss botanist who as a young man wrote a paper accurately describing the division of cells; he and Hugo von Mohl, a German botanist, first noted the differences between plant cell walls and their interiors

Glossary

botanical—substance taken from a plant

chlorophyll—green substance in plant cells that captures solar energy

clear-cutting—forestry management technique in which all trees in an area are cut down at the same time

decompose—to break down dead plants and animals into simpler substances

fertilizer—nutrients added to soil to make plants grow better

herbology—practice of using plants for medicine

leaf—green part of plants, attached to a stem, where photosynthesis occurs

organic—grown without using chemical pesticides

parasites—organisms that live in or on another organism for nourishment or protection

pesticides—substances used to kill pests

phloem—tiny tubes that carry food from the leaves to other parts of the plant

photosynthesis—process by which plants make food using sunlight, carbon dioxide, and water

radiation—energy in the form of rays or waves

renewable resource—source of energy, such as wind or sunlight, that can regenerate and will not run out

respiration—creation of energy in plants involving the exchange of oxygen and carbon dioxide

roots—parts of a plant that grow underground and absorb water and nutrients from the soil

selective cutting—removal of individual trees or small groups of trees in an area

solar energy—energy in sunlight

stalk—part of the plant that attaches the leaf to the stem

stems—parts of plants that support leaves, branches, and flowers

stomata—tiny holes in a plant that allow gases and water to enter and exit

veins—tiny tubes in a leaf that carry food

water cycle—process in which water evaporates from the ground, condenses in the atmosphere, and falls back to Earth

xylem—tiny tubes in a plant that carry water and nutrients from its roots to the leaves

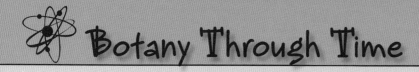

c. 8000 B.C. Humans begin cultivating crops

300s B.C. Greek philosopher Aristotle collects information about most of the known plants; his pupil Theophrastus creates the first system for classifying types of plants

1600s A.D. Using microscopes, scientists closely observe plant structures for the first time

1665 Robert Hooke publishes *Micrographia*, which describes his microscopic observations of plants

1671 Nehemiah Grew and Marcello Malpighi report the results of their microscopic studies of plants to the Royal Society of London

mid-1700s Swedish naturalist Carl Linnaeus creates a system for naming plants that becomes the standard classification system

1779 Jan Ingenhousz describes the results of his studies of plant functions; his experiments lead him to discover photosynthesis

1800 Jean Senebier demonstrates that photosynthesis begins when light strikes green plants

1817 Pierre-Joseph Pelletier and Joseph Bienaime Caventou create a pure form of chlorophyll

1831 Robert Brown discovers a structure in the cells of orchids and other plants that he calls the nucleus of the cells

1838 Matthias Schleiden discovers that all plant tissues are made of cells or cell-related materials

1866	Gregor Mendel publishes the results of his pea plant breeding experiments, which support his theory of genetic inheritance
1893	Charles Barnes coins the term photosynthesis to describe the process discovered a century earlier
1900	European scientists begin using Mendel's genetic theory to improve plant species by crossing plants of different varieties to produce the characteristics desired
1915	The Ecological Society of America is founded to promote the study of ecology, the science of the relationships between organisms and their environments
1960	Robert Woodward creates artificial chlorophyll
1961	Melvin Calvin wins a Nobel Prize for his studies of chemical reactions during photosynthesis
1985	Scientists create a device to measure plants' responses to environmental conditions, such as drought and pollution
1987	Genetically engineered crops (tobacco and tomato) are field tested for the first time in the United States
1992	The U.S. Department of Agriculture approves the production and sale of a genetically engineered tomato, but few consumers buy it
2009	By changing the genes in tobacco plants, European researchers say they have grown plants that could produce a powerful anti-inflammatory drug, interleukin-10, at low cost

Benbow, Ann, and Colin Mably. *Lively Plant Science Projects*. Berkeley Heights, N.J.: Enslow Publishers, 2009.

Johnson, Rebecca L. *Powerful Plant Cells*. Minneapolis: Millbrook Press, 2008.

Latham, Donna. *Respiration and Photosynthesis*. Chicago: Raintree, 2009.

Oxlade, Chris. *Solar Energy*. Chicago: Heinemann Library, 2008.

Stille, Darlene R. *Plant Cells: The Building Blocks of Plants*. Minneapolis: Compass Point Books, 2006.

Internet Sites

FactHound offers a safe, fun way to find Internet sites related to this book. All of the sites on FactHound have been researched by our staff.

Here's all you do:
    Visit *www.facthound.com*
FactHound will fetch the best sites for you!

Index

Michael L. Macceca

Michael Macceca received a degree in mammalian physiology and neuroscience and specialized in chemistry at the University of California at San Diego. He is currently a criminalist with the San Diego Sheriff's Crime Lab. He specializes in identifying trace evidence from explosives, fire debris, shoe prints, tire tracks, hair, fiber, and other tiny materials. He is the proud father of two budding scientists, Jack and Madeleine.

Image Credits